ADE ADEPITAN
A Paralympian's Story

Written by Ade Adepitan

Illustrated by
Philip Bannister

Contents

The green trees of Nigeria   2

The long road to school   6

A book a week   8

The Newham Rollers   12

Life in a chair   16

Training in the dark   20

Becoming a star in Spain   22

Training makes perfect   28

The Australian dream   30

TV, tigers and more training   34

Co-captain and more   38

A royal meeting   42

The trek of my life   44

London 2012   48

Glossary   52

Index   53

My life in sport and on TV   54

Collins

The green trees of Nigeria

I came to the UK from Nigeria when I was three years old. I'd contracted polio as a child of 15 months and my parents thought I would get better medical treatment in the UK.

My most distinctive memory of Nigeria is a recurring dream I used to have about these amazing green, lush trees. When I went back to Nigeria in 2007, I saw the trees when we were driving from the airport to my parents' home town and all the memories came flooding back to me.

Nigeria, in West Africa

Both of my parents are from Nigeria. They were
teachers there with good careers, but there was no
treatment for polio. I couldn't walk and they didn't
know if I was going to get worse. My dad felt
like he didn't have much choice, so we
said goodbye to all our friends and
family and moved
to east London.

3

Polio is a waterborne disease – you get it from polluted water and it affects a certain area of your spinal cord, which stops you from sending messages and growing muscles in certain parts of your body. I've got feeling in my legs but no movement. My left side is worse, but the degree of severity increases down my body. For example, it only affects my left hand a little bit – I can move it, but can't hold a pen with it.

When I came to the UK I was given a calliper splint to wear on my left leg. This consisted of iron rods strapped to my leg and which went into a big hospital medical boot – it definitely didn't look cool! Everyone else was wearing trainers and I was wearing these ugly brown boots. Plus, it was really uncomfortable, as the calliper splint didn't bend, so my left leg was dead straight when I sat down.

I could walk, but in a kind of robotic way. However, using a wheelchair was never really an option. If you could walk at all it didn't matter what you looked like, or how bad the pain was, walking was always encouraged. My parents really wanted me to walk and had a deep belief that with the support of the calliper and enough practice, I'd get better and would eventually walk on my own.

The long road to school

Schools in the UK at that time were separated into **mainstream schools** and disability schools. If you were disabled you went to a school for kids with disabilities – no matter what your disability was or how old you were. If you were **able-bodied**, you went to a mainstream school.

me as a child

My dad's intentions were for me to go to a mainstream school. He was so determined that eventually, after about a year of campaigning, one school finally accepted me. I was the first disabled kid in my area to go to a mainstream school and my parents saw it as a real achievement – a step in the right direction towards me having a normal life.

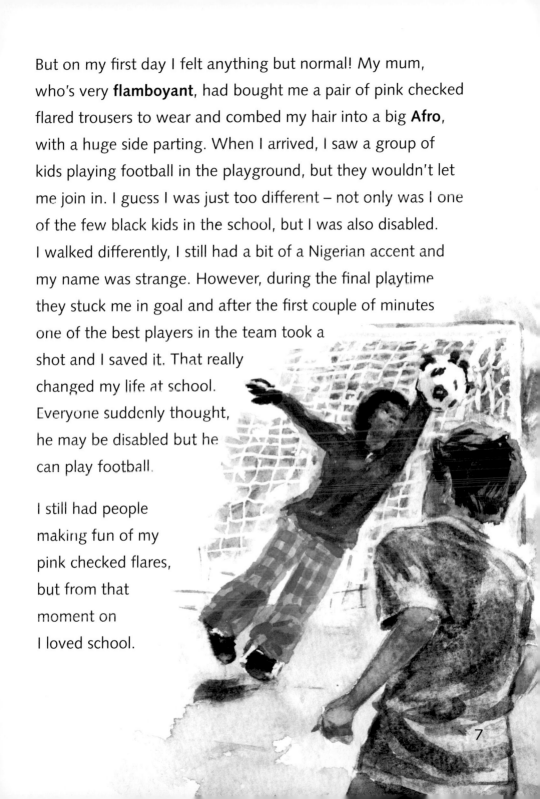

But on my first day I felt anything but normal! My mum, who's very **flamboyant**, had bought me a pair of pink checked flared trousers to wear and combed my hair into a big **Afro**, with a huge side parting. When I arrived, I saw a group of kids playing football in the playground, but they wouldn't let me join in. I guess I was just too different – not only was I one of the few black kids in the school, but I was also disabled. I walked differently, I still had a bit of a Nigerian accent and my name was strange. However, during the final playtime they stuck me in goal and after the first couple of minutes one of the best players in the team took a shot and I saved it. That really changed my life at school. Everyone suddenly thought, he may be disabled but he can play football.

I still had people making fun of my pink checked flares, but from that moment on I loved school.

A book a week

I was a really keen reader. Because my parents didn't allow me to play out much with the other kids in case I hurt myself, the only thing they really encouraged me to do was read. So I did – I read a book a week.

My parents always wore traditional Nigerian clothes. Here we all are just after we arrived in London.

We had quite a few problems in the area because we were the only African family and my parents were proudly African. They'd go to Nigerian parties, wear their Nigerian clothes and listen to Nigerian music, so we were seen as strange. I got teased a lot and hated the way we were treated, just for being different. It made me want to wear my English clothes so that I'd look like everybody else.

But it made my parents even more protective of me, so I spent a lot of time at home. Because of that, I was really pleased when we got our first TV – it was just in time for the Los Angeles Olympics in 1984. I would have been about 11 and the Games just totally blew me away. For those two weeks I was glued to the TV. I'd sit on the sofa with my eyes shut and when the gun went off I'd be pumping my arms, imagining I was running the race with the guys. I was just a sports freak. I loved sport, both watching and playing it.

Sebastian Coe running the 1,500-metre race in the 1984 Olympics

Carl Lewis winning the 100-metre race in the 1984 Olympics

The Newham Rollers

I didn't get into basketball until I was about 12 or 13
years old. There was a disabled school in the area, where
they'd set up a sports club and within that a wheelchair
basketball team called the Newham Rollers. At first I didn't
want to join. For a start, I didn't really think of myself
as being disabled, plus I had a perception of wheelchairs
as ugly, clunky things that said more about you than
helped you.

But in the end I went along and at the games I saw some
of the guys from the **GB** basketball team, who happened to
be training. I was amazed by the chairs they were using –
state-of-the-art funky wheelchairs – and they were flying up
and down the court, doing wheelies and all sorts.
The players were all really big, with massive arms – they
looked like athletes and were so cool. As they were going
past, one of them gave me a wink and I thought, that's it,
that's what I want to be – I want to be like these guys.
I was getting frustrated at school playing football, because
as everyone else was getting bigger it was harder and harder
for me to compete with them, so I decided to try wheelchair
basketball instead.

To play wheelchair basketball, players have to build up very strong arm muscles.

When I got in the chair, which I had to borrow from the club, I was so small that it felt like the basketball was the same size as me. I remember throwing it up to the net for the first time and it didn't even get close! I played in the junior championships anyway, but, surprise, surprise, we lost.

I had a strong sense of
pride and wasn't used
to losing. During the next
year I practised really hard.
I spent hours working on
my hand-eye co-ordination,
sitting on the floor at home
throwing a ball at the living
room wall and catching it.
I also got my own wheelchair.
When we went back to that
tournament the next year,
we reached the final.

Life in a chair

My parents were totally against me getting a wheelchair – they saw it as a step backwards and it horrified them. For them, the wheelchair was a clear sign that I was disabled, but for me, the only time that I felt disabled was when I tried to walk as normally as possible, because I couldn't do it.

Being at Secondary School was making everything harder because the building was so much bigger than my Primary School and there was a lot of walking just to get from one lesson to the next. It was so tiring that at the end of the day when I got home I'd need to sleep for an hour or so to recover.
Also, as I was getting bigger the calliper was rubbing into my leg, causing all sorts of problems and it was very painful. Eventually my doctor suggested I take the wheelchair that I used for basketball to school. My parents were so against this that my dad threw it out of the house. He was just so disappointed with what it represented. However, I still kept it, covered up in the garden.

Then one day I pushed myself to school in it. I was worried about getting bullied by the kids, but when I showed them all the wheelies and stuff that I could do, everyone loved it and I realised that it was alright. After that, I used the chair all the time.

Using the chair came naturally to me, so I quickly learnt how to climb up and down kerbs and stuff. Wheelchair basketball is all about the chair skills. You can teach yourself how to shoot just by doing thousands of shots, but learning how to make the chair and you work as one, that's the hard bit. I even started tinkering with it, changing and **adapting** it, angling the wheels so that the chair could turn faster.

As my skills improved, I moved from the Newham Rollers to a senior team, the Tottenham Tigers, who were in the second division of the national league and had **sponsorship**, a proper coach and training facilities. We trained every Thursday night and would have some amazing sessions, but it was all a secret because my parents hated me playing, so I'd tell them that I was going to study at a friend's house or going to the library. I didn't like lying to them, after everything they'd done for me, but it was the only way I'd be able to play – and I really wanted to play!

But as time went on I knew that if I had a hope of being called for the national team, I had to take my basketball more seriously and I couldn't do that and keep up with my studies. So at 17 I left school to try to get into the national team. I was selected to try out for the 1992 Barcelona Paralympics team.

Training in the dark

I was training all the time. I used my local sports centre late at night, when it was free. The lights would be off, so I had to practise in the dark, but I thought if I could shoot and dribble in the dark then when the lights were on I'd be even better!

The national team coach invited me to training so that he could watch me play – that's how the best 12 for the team are selected. I got down to the final 15, so missed out on the Barcelona Paralympics. However, because I was only 18, I knew there'd be other chances and I set myself the goal of getting to the Games in Atlanta, USA, in 1996. I thought that four years was plenty of time to become a good enough player to get into the team.

21

Becoming a star in Spain

I moved clubs again, this time to the Hackney Sparrows, and we were invited to play in a tournament in Spain. A lot of the senior guys couldn't go and I became the star of the team, winning the trophy for top scorer. When we got back home, my coach received a fax from the Spanish team asking to sign me up professionally.

It was only the second time I'd been abroad and I couldn't speak Spanish, but I knew I didn't have anything keeping me in London – I wasn't in the national team, after all. So I went out to Spain. At first it was really scary, as I was homesick and lonely, but after about four or five months things improved, especially as I picked up Spanish pretty quickly. It was a beautiful place and I made really good friends, so I stayed for two years.

Zaragoza, Spain

I was still trying to get into the national team, hoping to be selected for the Atlanta Paralympics as well as the European and World Championships. So I was flying back to the UK regularly and going through the selection process, but I didn't make it into any of the teams leading up to Atlanta.

Each time I got closer and closer, so, in the year before Atlanta, I decided to move back to the UK permanently in order to focus fully. I got a job as a wheelchair salesman, then trained every evening. I got down to the fourteenth player for Atlanta, which meant I'd just missed out. I was devastated. A year after that I failed to get into the European Championships team, then the World Championships team. I felt like I'd let everyone down, but a **fluke** win in a tournament in Cyprus, where I was playing with the Hackney Sparrows, gave me the courage to want to train for the national team again.

Training makes perfect

I started training six hours a day, six days a week, setting myself targets each week. If I reached the target I'd have Sunday off and if I didn't reach it I'd train on the Sunday. I spent time on the internet studying what the best players in the world were doing.

Finally, in April 2000 I got a letter through the post saying I'd been selected for the Great Britain team for Sydney 2000. It was the most amazing moment of my life.

The Australian dream

We left for the Sydney Paralympics two weeks before the
Games and stayed in a holding camp on the Gold Coast
of Australia with the GB team, so that we could get used
to the heat and prepare for the competition in the right
environment. I was on **cloud nine** – 15 years on from
watching the LA Olympics as an 11-year-old kid I was
finally there. It felt like a dream and even when I look back
at it now, it still feels like one.

I remember filing into the stadium for the opening ceremony and hearing this massive roar. You couldn't even see the people in the top tier because they were so tiny. The hairs were standing up on the back of my neck because it was so thrilling.

Sydney Paralympic opening ceremony, 15 September 2000

We'd train in the morning, but it wouldn't be a heavy session – more technical than fitness, working on plays, **tactics**, fine-tuning our shooting and making sure that everything was running smoothly, then we'd go to the game. The build-up for the game was really intense. We'd watch a video of the team we were playing in the morning, then the coach would go through the running order of our tactics and the style of play. Finally, the starting five players would be put on the board.

Because I was still a **rookie**, I didn't get into many starting fives and would come on as a **substitute** a lot. We did really well in the group stages and got through to the semi-finals, but then we lost to Canada. During the match to decide who'd win bronze, we lost to the USA and it was all over. I remember looking at the team and everyone was in tears. It was devastating, but had still been a fantastic experience. We had 19,000 people at our game and there were 5,000 people outside trying to get in. It was unbelievable playing in front of that many people.

Our whole team was so disappointed when the USA team won the match and we went away with bronze.

TV, tigers and more training

The year after the Sydney Games, my TV career really began to pick up. It had started before I went to Spain when I was asked to do a documentary called "Hoop Dreams", about me and my quest to become a professional basketball player in Spain. It did really well and got me noticed, so in 1999 I was asked to present a children's programme about endangered species called "Tiger Tiger". I'd never presented before, so was really nervous, but the producers were more worried about the physical side of things: trekking through the jungle, climbing up the sides of cliffs and ravines and living in the middle of nowhere in India.

But that didn't really worry me – in fact, it sounded pretty exciting, plus it was an opportunity to earn some money as I tried to qualify for the Sydney team. India was incredible. We were there for a week – living out in the jungle, trekking on elephants and finally, on the last day, we saw some tigers.

Then the BBC came to talk to me
about doing a wheelchair basketball
ink to show in-between programmes.
went through a few moves and the
producers were amazed by what I
could do, so they worked with me
over the course of two weeks to come
up with a series of dance moves.

t was the BBC's most popular link –
shown thousands of times a year and
s still the thing that I get stopped for
all over the world. Whatever I do,
'll always be remembered for it and
think it was this that made my dad
really proud of me.

Co-captain and more

But it wasn't just my TV career that was going well.
In 2002 we competed in the European and World
Championships. I was made co-captain of the GB team
for the World Championships. We won bronze at the
European and silver at the World, then we went to the
Athens Paralympics in 2004.

One of the things that I'm most proud about was the
coverage that the Paralympics got at Athens. TV coverage
of paralympic sports was still pretty limited, but because
I was working as a TV presenter, I'd spoken to my
producer about how wrong it was. So a
TV camera crew was sent to Athens
and followed our games every day
while we were out there.

We were playing the USA in the quarter finals and were losing by one point. I'd come on as a sub with five minutes to go, then, with only eight seconds left, I went on a drive to the basket. One of their players **fouled** me, totally wiping me out and taking me out of my chair. If you're fouled in the act of shooting you get two penalty shots. So, I was on the free throw line, knowing that if I didn't make it there probably wasn't enough time for us to come back and win the game.

A player in the other team tried to take the ball from me, but he pushed me too hard.

So I made the first shot to make it 59-all. It went in.
Then I took the next shot. It went in too, and my team
went mad, picked me up off the ground in my wheelchair
and it was just a crazy, crazy moment, one of the best of
my life.

We went on to win the bronze medal match against
the Netherlands.

celebrating our win

A royal meeting

Seven or eight months later, I received a letter that had the Prime Minister's seal on it – I'd been awarded an **MBE**.

I went to collect my medal with my mum, dad and brother.

Outside Buckingham Palace it was pretty emotional for us all – my dad was shaking with nerves and my mum was crying. It was an amazing experience, but probably more for them than for me. I was a bit disappointed that I didn't get to meet the Queen, as she wasn't there to give out the awards, although meeting Prince Charles was very cool.

The trek of my life

In 2005, I was asked to trek with a group of disabled people across Central America. Twelve of us, all with different disabilities, were going to trek from one side of Nicaragua to the other. We had to get our own water, make our own meals, set up our own camp and stuff like that. We had a guide who was a former **SAS** guy and one local guy.

It was probably the most amazing thing I've done in my life. It was unbelievable – it took us a month and I lost six kilograms in weight. There were two of us in wheelchairs and although we had specially-designed chairs with chunkier tyres to help us, they still kept falling apart. By the end of the trek, we'd had so many punctures that we ended up putting vine leaves in the tyres instead of air.

We'd trek every day for seven or eight hours, with the aim of travelling 10 to 12 kilometres in a day. We were primarily in thick rainforest, so we couldn't see more than three to four metres ahead and it was just nothing but trees, mud, broken leaves and these crazy howler monkeys cracking nuts from the trees.
Then about an hour before it got dark, we'd have to find somewhere close to a river to set up camp.
Then we'd get up at six o'clock the next morning and carry on trekking.

Towards the end of the trip we came across a 1,520-metre volcano. The first part of the climb was done on horseback and we reached what was called the shoulder of the volcano, which was way up in the sky. We set up camp there, but would have to go up the second part of the volcano in our chairs or on foot because it was too steep for the horses. The idea was that we'd start at six o'clock in the morning, as soon as first light came up, and we'd need to reach the top by two o'clock if we were to be back down before dark.

We set off in the morning, but after about an hour my group had only travelled 20 metres. It soon became evident that at the pace we were going, we were never going to get up the volcano in time. So I climbed out of my chair and crawled up the rest of the volcano on my backside – it took me six hours to get to the top. It was the most physically exhausting thing I've ever done. What made it harder was that the ground was hot because of the heat of the volcano. So as I was crawling up it was burning my hands and backside. When we got to the top you could look right into the volcano and it was awesome. We climbed back down, which took another seven or eight hours – but it was worth it.

London 2012

I was heavily involved in the UK bid for the 2012 Olympics and Paralympics, which was cool because I got to hang out with David Beckham, Daley Thompson and Sir Bobby Charlton. I was sitting with David Beckham in the hall as the announcement was made and we just went crazy. Everyone was jumping up and down, and when I returned I got to go to Buckingham Palace again – and this time I met the Queen!

The Beijing Games in 2008 were really the first time I did any commentating and up until the first match I was fine, but when I saw the team coming out on to the court, and I saw some of my old team-mates, who were like brothers to me, it really freaked me out. I just thought that I should be there – playing basketball had been such a huge part of my life that it was really tough not to be down there on the court.

But then as we started commentating it became easier. One of the toughest things for an athlete is how to deal with retirement. For 20 years of my life I was devoted to being an athlete, then suddenly I wasn't an athlete anymore and I didn't know who I was.

I went on to be a presenter for the London 2012 Paralympics. Being in the studio linking everything together was a fantastic experience, but being in the studio linking everything together for the TV coverage of the London 2012 Paralympics was a fantastic experience, especially knowing that I'd been privileged to play a part in bringing these amazing games to the UK.

It felt so exciting to finally meet the Queen. Here she is shaking hands with the athlete Cathy Freeman.

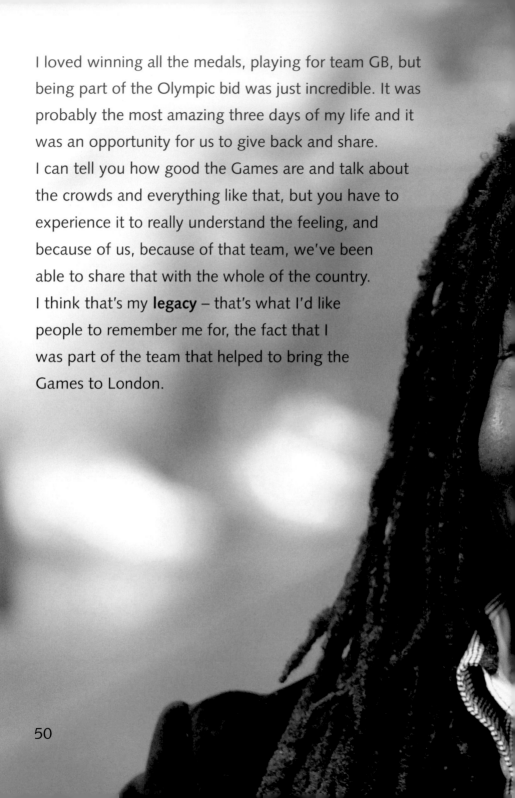

I loved winning all the medals, playing for team GB, but being part of the Olympic bid was just incredible. It was probably the most amazing three days of my life and it was an opportunity for us to give back and share.
I can tell you how good the Games are and talk about the crowds and everything like that, but you have to experience it to really understand the feeling, and because of us, because of that team, we've been able to share that with the whole of the country.
I think that's my **legacy** – that's what I'd like people to remember me for, the fact that I was part of the team that helped to bring the Games to London.

51

Glossary

able-bodied	not having a disability
adapting	making changes so as to improve something
Afro	curly hair
cloud nine	feeling very happy
flamboyant	wearing bright clothes that attract attention
fluke	unlikely and unexpected
fouled	been disadvantaged by an unfair tactic in sport
GB	Great Britain
legacy	something handed down to future generations
link	a connection between two things or people
mainstream school	an ordinary school
MBE	Member of the Order of the British Empire
rookie	person having their first full season in a sports team
SAS	Special Air Service (in the army)
sponsorship	money received from a person or organisation in return for advertising
substitute	a person taking the place of another in a game
tactics	special plans to improve games playing

Index

Athens Paralympics   38

Atlanta Paralympics   20, 26, 27

Barcelona Paralympics   19, 20

BBC   36

Beijing Paralympics   49

callipers   4, 16

Hackney Sparrows   22, 27

London Paralympics   48, 49, 50

MBE   42

Newham Rollers   12, 19

Nigeria   2, 3, 7, 9

polio   2, 3, 4

rookie   32

Spain   22, 24, 25, 34

Sydney Paralympics   29, 30, 31, 32, 33, 34, 35

Tottenham Tigers   19

training   12, 19, 20, 27, 28, 29, 32, 34

My life in sport and on TV

1973
I was born in Nigeria.

1974
I contracted polio.

1985
I discovered wheelchair basketball.

1990
I was selected to try out for the Barcelona Olympics.

1970   1980   1990

1976
I moved to London with my parents.

1991–1994
I won a tournament in Spain and took part in the TV documentary "Hoop Dreams".

1995
I tried out for the Atlanta Paralympics.

2000
I took part in the Sydney Paralympics.

2004
I took part in the Athens Paralympics and won a bronze medal.

2008
I commentated at the Beijing Paralympics.

2000 **2010**

2005
I trekked across Nicaragua, took part in the London 2012 Olympics bid and received the MBE.

2012
I commentated at the London Paralympics

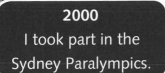

1999
I presented the TV programme "Tiger Tiger" and did a link for BBC TV.

Ideas for reading

Written by Clare Dowdall, PhD
Lecturer and Primary Literacy Consultant

Learning objectives: make notes on and use evidence from across a text to explain events or ideas; infer writers' perspectives from what is written and what is implied; identify how information texts are structured; plan and manage a group task over time using different levels of planning

Curriculum links: Citizenship

Interest words: adapting, calliper splint, flamboyant, fouled, legacy, mainstream schools, Paralympian, rookie, sponsorship, substitute, tactics

Resources: ICT, whiteboards

Getting started

- Read the title of the book together and help children to pronounce Ade Adepitan's name. Ask them to share what they know about the Paralympics and any famous Paralympians, based on their knowledge of the sporting event.

- Read the blurb and discuss how Ade Adepitan might have overcome his early illness to become a top sportsman and television presenter.

- Ask children to suggest what an autobiography is. Explain that an autobiography is a personal, factual account, written in the first person.

Reading and responding

- Read pp2–7 aloud to the group. Discuss how polio affected Ade, and how he felt about having to wear calliper splints. Using questions, support children to make simple inferences about Ade's first day at school, e.g. how did Ade feel when he was dressed in pink-checked flared trousers?

- Challenge children to read pp8–11, noting how Ade hated being treated differently to other children and families. Ask them to share their ideas about this and to relate feeling "different" to their own experiences.